WATERCOLOUR COURSE

A Step-by-Step Guide

Angela Gair

Abbeydale Press

This paperback edition printed in 2009

© 1996 Bookmart Limited

ISBN: 978-1-86147-200-7

5 7 9 10 8 6 4

Published by Abbeydale Press,
an imprint of Bookmart Limited,
Registered Number 2372865
Trading as Bookmart Limited, Blaby Road,
Wigston, Leicester, LE18 4SE, England

Originally published by Bookmart Ltd as part of
The Drawing and Painting Course in 1996
and as part of *The Artist's Handbook* in 1998

Printed in Thailand

WATERCOLOUR COURSE

A Step-by-Step Guide

Watercolour

AN INTRODUCTION TO
Watercolour

PROJECT 1

PROJECT 4

PROJECT 2

PROJECT 5

PROJECT 3

PROJECT 6

PROJECT 7

PROJECT 10

PROJECT 8

PROJECT 11

PROJECT 9

PROJECT 12

Watercolour

Watercolour is perhaps the most popular painting medium, with its unique delicacy and transparency capable of conjuring up the most fleeting and evanescent effects in nature. The fluidity of watercolour also makes it an exciting and unpredictable medium. For the inexperienced artist this element of uncertainty can be disconcerting at first, but a timid and cautious approach only results in a weak, dry, overworked painting. The secret of success with watercolour painting is to work boldly and with confidence. Once you learn to relax and let go of the reins, you will be delighted to find that very often the paint does much of the work for you; sometimes the most interesting and beautiful effects are achieved through a combination of accident and design. Watercolour may be occasionally irritating and frustrating, but it is never boring.

Materials and Equipment

One of the advantages of watercolour is that it requires few materials. All you need is a small selection of brushes, paints and papers and a jar of water, and you are ready to paint.

PAINTS

Watercolour paint consists of finely ground pigments bound with gum arabic and mixed with glycerine, which acts as a moisturiser. It is the translucence of the coloured washes that distinguishes watercolour from other media.

Choosing watercolour paints

There are two grades of watercolour – artists' and students'. The students' range is cheaper, but you will get better results from the artists' range, which contains finer quality pigments. The price is indicated by a series number. Some artists' colours are more expensive than others. Inorganic pigments, for example, can cost a lot more than the organic 'earth' colours.

Watercolour paints are available in tubes of thick, moist colour and in small blocks, called 'pans' or 'half-pans', of semi-moist colour.

Tubes

Tube colour is richer than pan colour and is useful for creating large areas of wash quickly; simply squeeze the paint onto a palette and mix it with water. It is best to squeeze out only a few colours at a time, keeping them well apart so that there is no danger of running together if you use too much water when mixing.

Right *A selection of tubes and pans of watercolour paint. These can be bought separately or in boxed sets of pre-selected colours.*

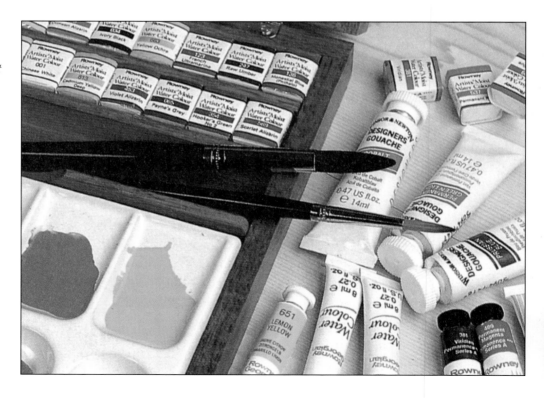

Pans

These small blocks of semi-moist colour can be bought individually as well as in special paint-boxes with slots to hold the pans in place and a lid that opens out to form a convenient mixing palette. They are economical to buy and useful for outdoor work as they are easily portable. However, it takes a little effort to lift enough colour onto the brush to make a large wash.

Gouache paints

Gouache is an opaque type of watercolour made by binding the pigments with gum arabic and combining them with white chalk. The paint dries to an opaque and slightly chalky matt finish, quite different to the delicate transparency of pure watercolour, but they can be diluted with water in the same way and applied with similar brushes.

BRUSHES

A common mistake beginners make when starting in watercolour is buying brushes that are too small. Because they can only make fine marks, their uses are limited. A large, good-quality brush is a better buy than several small ones because it holds plenty of paint for laying large washes and also comes to a fine point for painting fine details.

Choosing brushes

With watercolour brushes, it pays to buy the best you can afford. The better the brush, the better it performs and the longer it lasts. Cheap brushes are a false economy as they do not perform well and quickly wear out.
Sable brushes are the best choice for water-colour painting. They are expensive, but a pleasure to use, and if they are properly cared for they will last a long time. Springy, resilient and long-lasting, sable hair tapers naturally to a fine point.

Animal-hair brushes, made from ox, squirrel or goat hair, are also available. These are useful so long as a fine point is not required.
Synthetic-fibre brushes are a popular alternative to sable because they cost a lot less and are still quite springy and responsive. However, they don't hold the paint as well or last nearly as long. Also available are mixtures of synthetic and sable, which have good colour-holding and pointing properties.

Brush care

Look after your brushes and they will last you well. Never use a brush to scrub at the paint, and do not leave brushes standing in water while you work as this can ruin both the hairs

Below There are watercolour brushes to suit all purposes – and pockets. *A* flat wash brush. *B* round wash brush. *C* round synthetic brushes. *D* flat synthetic brushes. *E* mop brushes. *F* rigger brush. *G* round sable brushes. Water-colour sponges, *H*, are useful for applying broad washes and for lifting out colour.

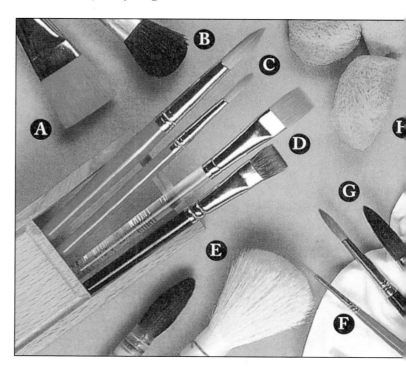

Left *When buying watercolour brushes, remember that quality is better than quantity. One good-quality sable brush, if looked after, will give you more years of service than a handful of cheap brushes.*

ideal for spreading water rapidly over the paper to create a wash. The flat edge is useful for making clean-cut lines.

Riggers are round with very long hair. They are designed to hold a lot of paint and produce thin, fine lines.

Mops and wash brushes are designed to paint large areas quickly. Wash brushes are wide and flat, while mops have large round heads.

Brush sizes

Brushes are graded according to size, ranging from as small as 0000 to as large as a no. 24 wash brush. The size of flat brushes generally denotes the width of the brush, measured in millimetres or inches. Brush sizes are not standardized, so a no. 6 brush in one manufacturer's range will not necessarily be the same size as a no. 6 in another.

PAPER

There is a wide selection of watercolour papers on the market, varying in texture, weight and quality. Which type you choose depends very much on your personal painting style and how much you want to spend. Start by buying single sheets of various types and try them out – you will soon discover which ones suit your way of working.

Watercolour paper can be either handmade or machine-made and this difference is reflected in the price. Ordinary cartridge paper, although good for drawing, is unsuitable for watercolour painting as it lacks strength and texture.

The best-quality handmade paper is made from

and the handles. Always rinse the brush in running water after use, making sure that any paint near the metal ferrule is removed. Then reshape it either by pulling it between your lips or by gently drawing it over the palm of your hand, moulding the hairs to a point. Stand your brushes, hairs uppermost, in a jar, or lay them flat. If you intend to store brushes in a box, make sure they are dry first, otherwise mildew may set in. Moths are very keen on sable brushes, so if you need to store them for any length of time, use mothballs to act as a deterrent.

Brush shapes

Rounds and flats (the flats are also called chisels or one-stroke brushes) are the main types of brush used for watercolour painting.

Rounds are bullet shaped brushes that come to a fine point. By moving the broad side of the brush across the paper you can paint broad areas of colour, and with the tip you can paint fine details.

Flats are wide and square-ended. They are

cotton rag instead of the usual woodpulp. Handmade papers are generally recognizable by their irregular surface and ragged ('deckle') edges. They also bear the manufacturer's water-mark in one corner. Mould-made papers are the next best thing to handmade, and are more affordable. Machine-made papers are the cheapest, but some have a rather mechanical surface grain.

Choosing paper

Watercolour paper can be bought in single sheets, but it is usually more economical to buy a spiral-bound pad. There are also watercolour blocks, which consist of sheets of pre-stretched paper gummed around the edges on all four sides; when the painting is finished and dry, the top sheet can be separated and taken off by running a palette knife along the edges.

Most watercolour paper is white or off-white, to reflect light back through the trans-parent washes of colour. However, tinted papers are also available, and these are often used when painting with body colour or gouache.

Paper texture

The surface texture of paper is known as its grain or 'tooth'. There are three kinds of surface:

Hot-pressed (HP) is smooth, with almost no 'tooth'. It is suitable for finely detailed work, but most artists find its surface too slippery for watercolour.

Not (meaning not hot pressed, and sometimes-referred to as 'cold-pressed') has a semi-rough

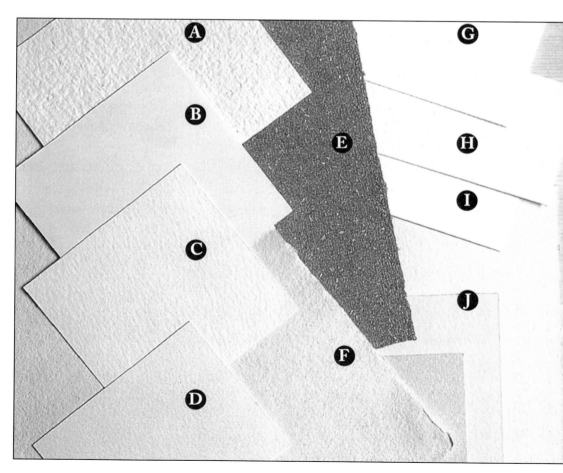

Right Try out different types of watercolour paper until you find one that suits you.
A Fabriano rough.
B Waterford hot-pressed.
C Waterford rough.
D Waterford Not surface.
E Handmade paper.
F Wilcox (cream).
G Bockingford Not surface.
H Whatman rough.
I Canson Montval Not surface.
J Bockingford tinted (shown here in grey, cream and eggshell).

Left For watercolour painting you will need a palette with deep wells that hold plenty of paint. Renew your water jar frequently to keep your colours fresh and clear.

metre (gsm). As a guide, the lightest water-colour paper is 70lb (150gsm), while a heavier paper is 140lb (285gsm). The heaviest paper weighs 300lb (640gsm).

Stretching watercolour paper

Lightweight watercolour papers – less than 140lb (285gsm) – should be stretched before use, to prevent them 'cockling' or buckling when paint and water are applied. Stretching is not usually necessary with heavier papers. To stretch paper, immerse the sheet in cold water for a couple of minutes (use a container large enough to take the sheet without being cramped – a sink or bath is best for large sheets). This expands the paper fibres. Hold the paper up by one corner to dislodge any surplus water, then lay it flat on a wooden board. Remove any air bubbles by rubbing briskly outward from the centre, using the backs of your hands.

Stick down the edges of the paper with strips of dampened gummed brown-paper tape, cut 2in (5cm) longer than the paper on each side. Leave to dry naturally. As the paper dries it shrinks and becomes as taut as a drum. Leave the gummed paper strips in place until the painting is completed and dry. Properly stretched paper will not buckle, even when flooded with washes.

surface equally good for vigorous washes and fine brush detail. This is the most popular type of surface for beginners.

Rough paper has a pronounced tooth which causes strokes and washes to break up. The paint sinks into the pitted surface and leaves tiny speckles of white paper untouched, causing the wash to sparkle with light.

Weight

Traditionally, the weight (thickness) of paper is measured in pounds per ream (480 sheets). The equivalent metric measure is grams per square

PALETTES

Watercolour palettes come in a range of shapes and sizes, and are made of either ceramic, enamelled metal or plastic. They are always white, which allows you to see the true colour of a wash with minimum distortion, and they all have recesses or wells that allow you to mix the paint with generous amounts of water.

Slant tiles These are rectangular ceramic palettes divided into several recesses or wells, allowing several colours to be laid out separately. The wells slant so that the paint collects at one end ready for use and can be drawn out of the well for thinner washes.

Tinting saucers are small, round ceramic dishes divided into four shallow compartments, each with a useful brush-rest on the edge. They are perfect for small-scale mixing, and also useful for holding masking fluid and watercolour mediums, to keep them separate from your colour mixes.

Cabinet saucers are the same as tinting saucers, without the divisions, and come with lids.

Palette trays These are usually made of plastic and have deep wells with plenty of room in each compartment to contain large amounts of fluid paint.

Improvised palettes Ordinary cups, bowls, plates and saucers – so long as they are white and non-porous – can be pressed into service as watercolour palettes. Hors d'oeuvres dishes are particularly useful as they provide several large mixing wells.

MEDIUMS

These are jellies and pastes that you can mix with your watercolour paints to alter their consistency, transparency and finish. Used in moderation, they allow you to achieve a variety of effects that are not normally possible with watercolours, while still retaining the basic translucent quality that is so characteristic of the medium.

Gum arabic is a pale-coloured solution that increases both the gloss and transparency of watercolours.

Ox gall liquid is useful for improving the flow and adherence of watercolours.

Acquapasto is a translucent jelly that thickens the consistency of watercolours to give an 'impasto' effect.

ACCESSORIES

You will need a well sharpened pencil for drawing; a kneaded putty eraser for erasing pencil lines without spoiling the surface of the paper; soft tissues for mopping up excess colour and lifting out colour to create highlights; a natural sponge for lifting out colour and for dabbing on areas of rough-textured paint; cotton buds for lifting out small areas of colour; jars for water; a wooden drawing board; gum-backed tape for attaching the paper to the board; and masking fluid for temporarily covering areas of the paper that you don't want to cover with paint.

Below Some of the accessories that you may find useful for creating specific textures and effects.

Using Masking Fluid

Alison Musker
RIO DI SAN LORENZO (detail)
To capture the faded grandeur of this old Venetian doorway, the artist applied ragged streaks of masking fluid to the paper before adding washes of colour on top. The paint adheres to the paper but not to the masked areas, creating a speckled pattern that suggests weathered stone and wood.

Because watercolour is a transparent medium it is impossible to paint a light colour over a dark one; you have to plan where the light or white areas are to be and paint around them. But suppose you are painting, for example, a seascape and you want to reserve small flecks of white paper to represent sparkling highlights on the surface of the water; attempting to apply broad, smooth washes while working around these tiny shapes can be a fiddly business. An effective solution is to temporarily seal off the white areas with masking fluid, allowing the rest of the surface to be painted over freely.

Masking fluid is a liquid, rubbery solution which is sold in bottles. Simply apply the fluid with a brush over the areas which are to remain white. Once it is dry (this takes only a minute or so) you can brush washes freely over the area without having to be careful to avoid the white shapes. When the painting is completely dry, the rubbery mask is easily removed by rubbing it off with your finger or with a clean eraser.

A word of warning – never allow masking fluid to dry on your brush as it will ruin it. Wash the brush in warm, soapy water immediately after use to prevent the rubber solution from drying hard and clogging up the bristles. It is a good idea to keep an old brush handy for applying masking fluid, or buy a cheap synthetic one specially for the purpose.

YOU WILL NEED

✔ *Stretched sheet of 140lb (285gsm) Not surface watercolour paper, 22 x 15in (55.8 x 38.1cm)*

✔ *Two old brushes (one small and one large) for applying masking fluid*

✔ *No. 12 round brush*

✔ *No. 3 round brush*

✔ *Masking fluid*

✔ *HB pencil*

✔ *Ruler*

Snow in Cape Cod

Masking fluid is essential for preserving small, intricate white shapes in a watercolour wash, leaving you free to paint over the masked areas. But you can also use it to retain large areas of the paper which need to be white – as in this winter scene, where blades of grass are peeping through the blanket of snow.

WATERCOLOUR PAINTS IN THE FOLLOWING COLOURS

● *French ultramarine*
● *Cobalt blue*
● *Payne's gray*
● *Yellow ochre*

● *Brown madder alizarin*
● *Raw umber*
● *Sap green*

1 Sketch out the scene with an HB pencil. If necessary, use a ruler to help you draw the horizontal lines of the wooden clapboarding on the front of the house. Mask out the window frames, using a small brush to apply the masking fluid. For the large patch of snow in the foreground, use a larger brush to apply masking fluid with broad, uneven diagonal strokes. Leave small gaps between the strokes; when painted, these will represent patches of grass peeping through the blanket of snow. Leave the masking fluid to dry for approximately 10 minutes.

Helpful Hint
TO AVOID THE RISK OF DAMAGING YOUR BEST WATERCOLOUR BRUSHES, USE OLD BRUSHES, OR CHEAP SYNTHETIC ONES, FOR APPLYING MASKING FLUID.

2 For the sky, mix a bright blue wash made up of cobalt blue heavily diluted with water. Apply this with broad, diagonal strokes using a no. 12 round brush, leaving patches of untouched paper to represent the clouds. Soften some of the cloud edges with a damp brush. Paint the glass in the windows with the same wash, using a no. 3 round brush.

3 Mix a very light, watery wash of Payne's gray warmed with a touch of yellow ochre and apply this to the front of the house and the bell tower on the roof with a no. 3 round brush.

4 For the brick detailing at the base of the house walls mix a light wash of brown madder alizarin and yellow ochre. Use the same colour mix to paint the chimney on the left. Paint the roof with a diluted wash of Payne's gray.

5 Paint the gable ends and the shadows on the bell tower with Payne's gray. For the shadows under the roof and under the windows use a pale blue-grey mixed from French ultramarine with just a little Payne's gray. Suggest the pattern of the brickwork on the walls and chimney using a mixture of brown madder alizarin and yellow ochre, darkened with a touch of raw umber. Apply the paint with short horizontal strokes, leaving tiny gaps to show the pattern of the bricks.

6 Mix a dark wash of Payne's gray and add some texture to the roof with a series of fine, closely spaced horizontal lines. Paint the fence with a heavily diluted wash of Payne's gray warmed with a little raw umber. Use the same wash, but less diluted, to pick out the windows on the bell tower. For the grass in the foreground, prepare a wash of yellow ochre, sap green and raw umber. Using a no. 12 round brush, apply the wash over the masking fluid using broad brushstrokes. The masking fluid will resist the paint, protecting the paper underneath. Leave until thoroughly dry.

7 Paint the fir trees in the foreground with sap green, raw umber and Payne's gray, changing the proportions of the colours in the mix to give variation to the greens. Use the tip of the brush to create the effect of leaves and thin branches. Notice how the foliage is darker towards the base of the trees glimpsed through the fencing. For the trees in the distance, use raw umber and a touch of sap green. Leave the painting to dry.

8 When the painting is completely dry you can remove the masking fluid. Rub firmly over the masked areas with your fingertip (make sure your hands are clean and free from grease) until the rubbery mask comes away, revealing the white paper beneath. Here you can see how the green paint has settled in the gaps left in the mask in step 1, giving the effect of patches of grass in the melting snow.

9 Use the same wash, but with a little cobalt blue and a lot more water added, to touch in the dark reflections in the windows. To finish, pick out the top edge of the brick detailing with a darker mix of the same wash. Leave the painting to dry thoroughly, then define some of the lines between the clapboard panels using an HB pencil.

Helpful Hint
IF YOU MAKE A MISTAKE WHEN APPLYING MASKING FLUID, SIMPLY WAIT FOR IT TO DRY AND THEN RUB IT OFF WITH YOUR FINGERTIP OR AN ERASER AND START AGAIN.

10 To complete the painting, mix a dark wash of sap green, raw umber and Payne's gray and work back over the trees with the no. 3 round brush, leaving some of the lighter green wash showing through.

Working Light to Dark

Trevor Chamberlain
SHADED BEACH, BEER
The impression of sparkling light in this painting is achieved by brushing thin, transparent washes onto dampened paper and letting them settle undisturbed. Light reflects off the white paper and up through the colours, giving them a marvellous luminosity.

With an opaque medium such as oil paint you can build up dark and light areas in any order. But because watercolour is transparent, light colours cannot be applied over dark ones; if you make a colour too dark in the first instance, it is difficult and messy to correct afterwards. The best method is to start off with the lightest of washes and build up gradually in a series of further washes to the density you require, leaving uncovered any areas that are to be left as white highlights.

The process of overlaying transparent washes results in richer, more resonant passages than can be achieved by painting with a single, flat wash of dense colour; light seems to reflect through each layer of colour, almost giving the appearance of being lit from within.

Drying

This technique requires a little patience because it is essential to allow each layer of paint to dry before applying the next; if you do not, the colours will simply mix and the crispness and definition will be lost. You can use a hairdryer to speed up the process, but avoid using it on really wet paint as it could blow your carefully placed wash all over the paper.

Testing colours

The characteristic freshness and delicacy of watercolour is lost if there is too much over-painting. Always test a colour on scrap paper before committing it to the painting, then apply it quickly, with one sweep of the brush, so that it does not disturb the paint below. A few layers of colour applied with confidence, will be more successful than colours muddied by constant reworking.

Reserving white areas

Working from light to dark means you have to establish where the lightest areas are at the outset and preserve them as your painting progresses. It is possible to remove paint by lifting out with a damp brush or sponge, but you can rarely retrieve the pristine whiteness of the paper with this method because the pigment usually sinks into the fibres of the paper and leaves a faint stain. It is wise therefore to start with a light pencil drawing to establish the correct position and shape of the highlights to be reserved. Small or awkwardly shaped highlights which are too difficult to work around can be preserved by masking them out with masking fluid prior to painting.

Shirley Trevena
WHITE LILIES AND PINK ROSES
Surrounded by dark tones in the background, these pure white lilies appear particularly striking. If you look closely, you will see that in fact the 'white' petals consist mainly of very thin translucent washes of warm and cool grey; white paper is reserved only for the brightest highlights.

Black Grapes, White Lace

Working from light to dark is the classical method of building up a watercolour painting. In this demonstration you will learn how to apply overlapping strokes and washes of transparent colour in order to create a convincing impression of three-dimensional form.

YOU WILL NEED

✓ *Sheet of 140lb (285gsm) Not surface watercolour paper 17 x 13.5in (43.2 x 34.3cm)*

✓ *No. 3 round brush*

✓ *No. 5 round brush*

WATERCOLOUR PAINTS IN THE FOLLOWING COLOURS

- *Raw sienna*
- *Prussian blue*
- *Alizarin crimson*
- *Sap green*
- *Cerulean*

- *French ultramarine*
- *Cadmium lemon*
- *Cadmium yellow*
- *Viridian*
- *Raw umber*

1 Use a dilute mix of raw sienna and French ultramarine to position the plate and the main folds in the cloth with a no. 3 round brush. Mix a thin wash of ultramarine, Prussian blue, alizarin crimson and a spot of sap green to make a grey-purple and start painting the grapes, leaving white paper for the light parts. Build up the darker tones with overlaid washes, adding a little cerulean blue in places. Add more Prussian blue and alizarin crimson to the wash and paint the dark shapes between the grapes.

Helpful Hint
IF YOU MAKE A MISTAKE, FLOOD THE AREA WITH WATER AND THEN BLOT OFF THE OFFENDING PAINT WITH CRUMPLED TISSUE OR A CLEAN BRUSH.

2 With the same light and dark washes used in step 1, continue to define the rounded forms of the grapes. Work methodically from light to dark, painting carefully around the sharpest highlights. Define the outline of the plate and deepen the shadow beneath it with a thin mix of Prussian blue, ultramarine, raw sienna and a touch of alizarin crimson. Soften the edge of the shadow using a damp brush.

3 Continue building up the darks on the grapes, deepening the grey-purple mix with a little raw sienna in places. This method of working from light to dark is very effective – the grapes look luscious enough to eat! Now pick out the pattern on the plate with cerulean blue and give more definition to the rim with the same grey-

blue wash used earlier. Loosely outline the stray group of grapes on the cloth with the same pale wash used in step 1. In the detail (right) we see how the artist models the forms of the grapes with small, curved brushstrokes applied wet-on-dry. With the dark tones in place, the small flecks of bare paper read as bright, shiny highlights.

4 Continue painting the grapes in the foreground, using the same colour mixes used for the main bunch and leaving tiny white highlights. Now mix up a very dilute wash of raw sienna, ultamarine and a little burnt umber and put in more of the folds in the cloth with the no. 5 brush. Define its lacy edging by painting the shadows it casts. Use a darker version of the same wash to pick out the tiny decorative holes in the cloth with the tip of the no. 3 brush.

5 Paint the buttercup with mixtures of cadmium lemon and cadmium yellow, leaving tiny flecks of white paper for the highlights on the shiny petals. Paint the leaves and stem with sap green, alizarin crimson and just a touch of viridian. Apply clean water over the area of the green cloth using the no. 5 brush. Mix a light wash of sap green, cerulean and cadmium yellow and brush this onto the wet paper with broad, sweeping strokes.

6 Switch to the no. 3 brush and add the darkest tones to the small group of grapes with a dark blue-purple mix of Prussian blue, raw sienna, cerulean and raw umber. Paint the stalk with a darker version of the green used for the buttercup stalk. Go back to the lace, working on the edge in the foreground. Vary the sizes and tones of the holes to describe the folds in the fabric and the soft shadows falling across its surface.

7 To finish, darken the shadows round the edges of the lace cloth using a mix of Prussian blue, raw sienna and just a touch of alizarin crimson. Use the same wash but with more water added to go over the shadows in the cloth to emphasize the shadowy folds in the fabric.

Painting Wet-in-Wet

Trevor Chamberlain
BEFORE BALLET CLASS *In this charming study soft, diffused washes perfectly capture the gauzy, semi-transparent fabric of the ballet dancers' tutus.*

Wet-in-wet is one of the most beautiful and expressive techniques in watercolour painting. When colours are applied to a wet or damp surface they merge gently into each other and dry with a soft, hazy quality. This is particularly effective in painting skies and water, producing gentle gradations of tone that evoke the ever-changing quality of the light.

Subjects

The wet-in-wet technique is particularly effective when painting large expanses of soft colour, for example in skies and misty landscapes, producing gentle gradations of tone and hue that capture the ever-changing quality of

outdoor light. When painting delicate or hazy subjects such as flowers, fruits and distant landscape elements, wet-in-wet allows the colours to blend naturally on the paper without leaving a hard edge.

Preparation

For this technique it is best to use a heavy-grade paper (200lb/410gsm or over) which will bear up to frequent applications of water and paint without wrinkling. Lighter papers will need to be stretched and firmly taped to a board. Moisten the paper with water using a large brush or soft sponge. Blot off any excess water with a tissue so that the paper is evenly damp, with no water lying on the surface. Tilt the board at a slight angle so that the colours can flow gently down the paper; if it is laid flat there is a danger of washes creeping backwards and creating unwanted marks and blotches, known as 'blooms'.

Painting method

Working wet-in-wet requires confidence because you can only control the paint to a certain extent. Large brushes work best as they hold plenty of paint and enable you to lay in broad sweeps of colour. Charge your brush fully and work quickly and lightly, allowing the colours to spread and diffuse of their own accord. A common mistake when working wet-in-wet is to dilute the colour too much, with the result that the finished painting appears weak and insipid. Because the paper is already wet you can use quite rich paint – it will soften on the paper but retain its richness. You must also compensate for the fact that the colour will dry lighter than it appears when wet.

Make sure you mix plenty of paint – there is nothing more frustrating than running out of colour halfway through and having to stop to mix some more!

Michael Chaplin
THE ITALIAN ALPS
This is another example of the skilful use of the wet-in-wet technique, used in a robust manner to capture the atmosphere of mist and rain in the mountains.

Flowers in Blue Jar

This delightful jug of flowers is more a lyrical impression of the subject than a literal interpretation. The artist worked rapidly and intuitively, flooding the colours onto wet paper to create softly blended, hazy colours that merge and flow into one another. It is an exciting method of watercolour painting as the results are unpredictable, but also highly expressive.

YOU WILL NEED

✔ Stretched sheet of 140lb (285gsm) Not surface watercolour paper, 17½ x 22in (44.4 x 55.8cm)

✔ No. 16 round brush

✔ No. 5 round brush

✔ Drinking straw

✔ Table salt

WATERCOLOUR PAINTS IN THE FOLLOWING COLOURS

- Indigo
- French ultramarine
- Alizarin crimson
- Winsor blue
- Winsor green
- Hooker's green dark
- Cadmium yellow
- Permanent white

1 Tilt your board at a slight angle, then wet the entire sheet of paper with clean water using a no. 16 round brush. With the same brush, and working quickly, drop in separate blobs of colour to suggest flower heads. Use indigo for the blue-purple flowers, alizarin crimson mixed with a little indigo for the deep purple flowers and diluted alizarin crimson for the pink flower heads. Mix French ultramarine with indigo for the blue background areas and, for the foliage, use Hooker's green dark mixed with indigo. The colours will spread and merge on the wet surface, leaving lighter areas in between that suggest tiny white flowers.

Helpful Hint

SPEED IS CRUCIAL WHEN WORKING WET-IN-WET, SO HAVE YOUR WASHES READY-MIXED IN DEEP-WELLED PALETTES OR SAUCERS BEFORE YOU START PAINTING. REMEMBER TO MIX UP PLENTY OF PAINT SO YOU DON'T RUN OUT AT AN INCONVENIENT MOMENT.

2 Move quickly across the painting, adding dabs of ultramarine, alizarin and indigo and cutting around the shapes of the white flowers. Speed is essential – the paper must be wet enough to allow the colours to spread. Don't attempt to paint the flowers realistically – let your intuition and imagination be your guide. Use the tip of the brush to give an impression of the forms of leaves and petals. Define the form of the jug by painting around it with a diluted wash of French ultramarine.

3 Put in some darks behind the group to give it definition. Use various combinations of indigo, Winsor blue and ultramarine. Mix Winsor blue and indigo and deepen the tones around the jug. With a stronger mix of the same colour, indicate the shadow cast by the jug to anchor it to the table. This detail shows the use of a clever 'trick of the trade'. Sprinkle a few grains of salt into the wet wash and leave to dry for 10 minutes. The salt absorbs the paint, leaving tiny, pale star shapes which add subtle texture and suggest small white flowers.

4 Brush some water over the large pink flower and drop in a darker wash of alizarin crimson and a little indigo to add tonal contrast. Describe the petals with the tip of the brush and add soft-edged highlights by sprinkling on a little salt to absorb the paint. Leave to dry, then mix a wash of alizarin and indigo and add some dark flowers and foliage for contrast.

5 Paint the jar with a strong aquamarine mixed from Winsor blue and Winsor green, letting the colour fade out towards the edges. Paint the shadow on the right with ultramarine and indigo; let the colour diffuse softly into the aquamarine wash, describing the rounded form of the jar. Enrich the shadow on the table with a loose wash of ultramarine and indigo.

6 Use a mix of Winsor green, Winsor blue and indigo to suggest the dark foliage on the left edge of the arrangement with loose brushstrokes. Using the same mix, suggest a few seed heads by dabbing on the paint with your fingertip to make small blots and using a drinking straw to 'paint' the dried stalks (see detail). To create the delicate stalks carrying the seed heads, place one end of a drinking straw over the wet blots of paint and gently blow through the other end, to send tiny trails of paint spreading outwards.

7 With a no. 5 round brush, paint the dark centres of the flowers at the front of the arrangement. Use a little white gouache paint to pick out the tiny white daisies at the top right, and to define the nearer white flowers at the bottom left. Paint the centres of the daisies with cadmium yellow.

8 Add some crisp touches to the nearer flowers to bring them forward. Mix alizarin and a touch of indigo and dot in the stamens and centres of the large daisies using the tip of your brush. Finally, use a light tone of indigo to suggest veins on some of the leaves.

Painting Water

Trevor Chamberlain
THAMES REFLECTIONS
Capturing the smooth, light-reflecting surface of calm water means keeping your colours fresh and clear and letting your brush-strokes and washes settle undisturbed.

Lakes, rivers, streams and ponds are attractive but elusive subjects, being constantly on the move: ripples and eddies come and go; colours change; reflections stretch and shrink; waves break and re-form before you have a chance to put brush to paper. It is easy to become confused and end up including too much detail in your painting, with the result that the water looks more like a patterned carpet!

The secret of painting water is to seek out the major shapes of light and dark and omit all superfluous details; water looks wetter when painted simply. You've probably heard the saying 'less is more', and nowhere does this apply more readily than in the painting of water. Achieving the smooth, glassy appearance of calm water requires surprisingly little effort; often just a few sweeping strokes with a broad brush on damp paper are enough to convey the illusion.

Painting methods

Watercolour has a unique transparency and freshness which is ideally suited to painting water. Broad, flat washes are ideal for conveying the still surface of a lake or river, and a broken, drybrush stroke dragged across rough white paper is a wonderfully economical means of suggesting highlights or patches of wind-ruffled water in the distance. Masking fluid is useful here, as you can block out small high-lights on the water's surface while you work freely on the surrounding washes.

Try brushing your colours directly onto dampened paper and letting them merge together wet-in-wet for a soft, diffused impression of a misty lake. Ripples and reflections can be described in a kind of shorthand with calligraphic brushmarks and squiggles, letting the action of your brush suggest the water's undulating movement.

Reflections

If you remember that reflections obey certain laws of perspective, you will find it easier to paint them convincingly. For example, you will notice that the reflection of a light object is always slightly darker than the object itself – and vice versa. An object standing upright in the water produces a reflection of the same length, but the reflection of an object leaning towards you appears longer, and that of an object leaning away from you appears shorter. When the water's surface is disturbed, reflections break up and appear longer than the object reflected. These broken reflections, too, follow the laws of perspective; as they recede into the distance they gradually appear smaller, flatter and more closely spaced.

Dennis Gilbert
ISLE OF WIGHT
Here the effect of sunlit surf is skilfully created by skimming the brush lightly over the paper to create broken strokes and leaving small flecks of the white paper unpainted.

Canal in Amsterdam

In this Dutch canal scene the water's surface is ruffled by a breeze, causing the reflections to stretch and distort and form fascinating patterns. These reflections have been freely painted, with calligraphic lines and squiggles that suggest the way they are broken up by the gentle movement of the surface of the water.

YOU WILL NEED

✓ *Sheet of 140lb (285gsm) Not surface watercolour paper, 22 x 15in (55.8 x 38.1cm)*

✓ *No. 10 round brush*
✓ *No. 8 round brush*
✓ *No. 3 round brush*
✓ *HB pencil*

WATERCOLOUR PAINTS IN THE FOLLOWING COLOURS

- *Naples yellow light*
- *Cobalt blue*
- *Yellow ochre*
- *Raw umber*
- *Brown madder alizarin*
- *Sap green*
- *Payne's grey*

1 Lightly sketch in the main elements of the scene with an HB pencil. Mix a weak solution of Naples yellow light and apply this over the whole painting, except for the water, with a no. 10 round brush. For the water, mix an equally weak solution of cobalt blue. Leave to dry.

Helpful Hint

REMEMBER THAT WET WATERCOLOUR LOOKS DECEPTIVELY STRONG AND WILL DRY LIGHTER. IF YOU USE TOO LITTLE PIGMENT WITH TOO MUCH WATER, YOUR PAINTING WILL LOOK INSIPID.

2 Paint the lightest tones on the stone bridge and its reflection in the water with a mixture of yellow ochre and raw umber. Use the same colour for the stone ledge on the far right of the picture. Leave to dry.

3 Mix a slightly darker wash of raw umber and yellow ochre and, using a no. 8 round brush, paint the stone detailing along the top of the bridge. Then paint the detailing around the arches, dragging the colour down into the water with wavering strokes to describe the reflections. Leave to dry.

4 Mix a wash of brown madder alizarin and raw umber to make a warm, pinkish brown for the brickwork on the bridge and its reflection in the water. Again, use smooth, wavering strokes to show how the reflections break up on the rippling surface. Using the same wash, and the wash used in step 3, suggest some of the details of trees and buildings in the background, glimpsed over the top of the bridge.

5 Using a no. 3 round brush, paint the grassy bank behind the arch on the left with a pale tone of sap green and raw umber. For the reflections seen through the same arch use a wash of sap green, raw umber and brown madder alizarin. Paint the dark shadows inside the arches with a mix of brown madder alizarin and Payne's gray. Drag the washes down into the water, then pull some of the wet paint out at the edges to create the broken reflections, as shown.

6 Paint the delicate shapes of the trees in the background using a mixture of sap green and a little raw umber for the foliage and raw umber for the trunks and branches. Dilute the colours to a pale whisper, otherwise the trees will jump forward and look as if they are sitting on top of the bridge instead of behind it. Then mix raw umber and yellow ochre for the stone slabs on the ledge on the right. Note how the slabs become cooler and lighter in tone as they recede into the distance.

Helpful Hint
ALWAYS LET ONE WASH DRY BEFORE PAINTING OVER IT. IF YOU ARE IMPATIENT AND ATTEMPT TO PAINT ON TO DAMP WASH YOU MAY CREATE STREAKS AND RUNS THAT RUIN THE EFFECT OF SMOOTH, CLEAR WATER.

7 Mix a deeper version of the wash used in step 4 and use this to suggest the pattern of the brickwork on the bridge. Apply the paint with short, horizontal strokes, leaving tiny gaps between them. Use the same wash to darken the reflection of the bridge in the water. Leave the painting to dry.

39

8 Draw pencil lines to define the individual stone slabs around the arches. Build up the forms of the background trees using different strengths of sap green and raw umber. Work back over the dark areas inside the arches using the same mix you used in step 5, darkened with more Payne's gray. Resume work on the reflections beyond the lefthand arch with brown madder alizarin and raw umber.

Helpful Hint
ALWAYS HAVE TWO JARS OF WATER WHEN WORKING IN WATERCOLOUR – ONE OF CLEAN WATER FOR LOADING BRUSHES AND WETTING THE PAPER, AND ONE FOR RINSING BRUSHES WHILE YOU WORK.

9 Mix brown madder alizarin and raw umber and paint the shadow under the stone ledge along the top of the bridge. Then mix a darker wash of brown madder alizarin and Payne's gray for the dark lines at the base of the bridge, just above the water line. Paint the darker ripples in the blue water with brushstrokes of cobalt blue, slightly deeper in tone than the original wash, to suggest the reflection of the sky.

10 Make a dark, brownish black from Payne's gray and raw umber and use the tip of your brush to paint the delicate shapes of the railings. Dilute the wash to a pale grey for the railings on the far side of the bridge, and for the bicycles.

11 Complete the painting by putting in the reflections of the bicycles and the railings using the mixes used in step 10, but warmed slightly with a little brown madder alizarin. Use fluid, calligraphic strokes applied quickly and confidently, to suggest the distortions created by the movement on the water's surface.

Using Gum Arabic

Sarah Donaldson
THE GARDEN GATE
In this rapidly executed watercolour sketch the addition of gum arabic adds richness and texture to the paint so that the lively brush-work is enhanced.

Gum arabic is derived from the sap of tropical acacia trees and has been used for centuries as a binder in the manufacture of watercolour paints. It can also be obtained as a bottled liquid for use as a painting medium. When added to watercolour paint in the palette, it enlivens the texture of the paint and enhances the vividness of the colours.

Because it also slows down the drying time of the paint, gum arabic can give greater versatility to your watercolours allowing you to keep the paint fluid on the surface for longer, work into it and create textural effects.

Paint mixed with gum arabic can be dissolved easily even when dry, because the gum suspends the pigment and prevents it from soaking into the paper. This makes it particularly useful if you want to lift out colour to create highlights. Add just a tiny drop of gum arabic to the dilute paint in your palette, or add some to the water in your jar. Don't use too much, otherwise the paint becomes slippery and jelly-like.

Gum arabic can also be used as a kind of varnish. Once the finished painting is thoroughly dry you can brush a thin layer of diluted gum arabic over it which dries with a slightly glossy surface which imparts a rich lustre to the colours. It should never be used undiluted, however, as it will crack in time.

Tropical Fruit

YOU WILL NEED

- ✔ Sheet of 140lb (285gsm) rough watercolour paper 12 x 9in (30.5 x 22.8cm)
- ✔ Ox gall
- ✔ Gum arabic
- ✔ Medium-sized Oriental brush
- ✔ No. 4 round brush
- ✔ HB pencil

WATERCOLOUR PAINTS IN THE FOLLOWING COLOURS

- Cobalt blue
- Prussian blue
- Aurora yellow
- Rose madder
- Chinese white

In this still life, transparent washes of colour have been worked over one another in order to build up a strong sense of form in the fruits. The addition of gum arabic and ox gall gives a new dimension to the paint and an opportunity to develop texture and tone

1 Sketch the main outlines of the composition using an HB pencil, but don't add any detail at this stage. Ensure that the fruits are in correct proportion to each other and that the composition is well set out in relation to the edges of the paper; here, the artist has chosen an overhead viewpoint to create a striking composition, with the top of the vase just breaking the edge of the table top.

Helpful Hint

ORIENTAL BRUSHES ARE GREAT FOR WATERCOLOUR PAINTING AS THEY HOLD PLENTY OF PAINT FOR LAYING WASHES, YET COME TO A FINE POINT FOR DETAILS.

2 Block in the background area with a pale wash of aurora yellow, applied loosely with a medium-sized Oriental brush. Add a patch of the same colour on the vase to suggest the reflection of the grapefruit on its shiny surface. Then block in all the fruits, leaving patches of white paper for the highlights. For the kumquats, add a little rose madder to the wash to make a pale orange. For the blue-green tones of the vase, mix a well-diluted wash of Prussian blue and cobalt blue, leaving a small patch of bare paper for the highlight.

3 When the first washes have dried, start to model the rounded forms of the vase and fruits with darker tones. Apply thin washes of cobalt blue mixed with aurora yellow to add greenish tones to the grapefruit, lemon, starfruit, lime and prickly pear, concentrating on the shadow areas. Loosely wash the same colour over the background, then paint the shadows beneath the fruits.

Helpful Hint

OX GALL IS ANOTHER USEFUL WATER-COLOUR PAINTING MEDIUM. IT IS A PALE-COLOURED LIQUID WHICH INCREASES THE FLOW OF WATERCOLOUR PAINT. AS WITH GUM ARABIC, USE IT SPARINGLY.

4 Introduce warmer tones to the fruits with various mixtures of aurora yellow, rose madder and a little cobalt blue, adding wash over wash in the shadows to build up three-dimensional form. Brush a small amount of ox gall over the background area, then brush in some of the same warm colours, letting them blend wet-in-wet with the previous wash. This unifies your painting by linking foreground and background. With a no. 4 round brush, deepen the cast shadows with cobalt blue and Prussian blue.

5 Gradually add more pigment to the basic washes and work on the darker tones in the group, adding variety to the range of tints in the painting and giving a sense of light hitting the subject from the side. Notice how the objects pick up and reflect the colours around them: the reflection of the grapefruit in the vase, for example, and the subtle tinge of yellow in some of the shadows.

6 Concentrate on the shadows, building up transparent layers of colour one over the other. Mix a brushful of gum arabic with the paint for the darker tones; this adds body to the paint, enabling you to apply it in distinct brush strokes to suggest form and texture. It also gives the dark tones depth and luminosity, preventing them from becoming muddy. Leave to dry, then use a little of the grey shadow mixture to suggest the knobbly texture of the prickly pear.

7 Develop the darks and mid tones that describe the rounded form of the vase with transparent overlays of cobalt blue and Prussian blue, adding aurora yellow for the greenish tones. Add a little rose madder to the wash, plus some gum arabic to make the paint thicker and more controllable when painting small details. Use this to strengthen the small areas of deep shadow where the objects overlap. Mix a strong solution of rose madder and aurora yellow to strengthen the warm shadows on the kumquats.

Helpful Hint

TO GIVE A SENSE OF DEPTH TO THE PITCURE, USE SLIGHTLY STRONGER TONES AND COLOURS FOR THE OBJECTS AT THE FRONT OF THE STILL-LIFE GROUP, TO BRING THEM FORWARD.

8 To complete the painting, use a little Chinese white to highlight certain areas of the subject, giving the effect of reflected light. You can also use white at this stage to correct any areas of the painting you are not entirely happy with. Stand back from the picture to check that the perspective is working and that the background objects appear to recede on the picture plane. You may want to add warmer tints to the foreground objects to bring them forward.

Complementary Colours

Jane Camp
SUMMER'S DAY
The effect of complementary colours need not always be bright and strident. In this lyrical scene, the complementary blue-violets and yellows give a shimmering effect of sunlight, but because the colours have been lightened with Chinese white they have a quiet harmony.

Any two colours diagonally opposite each other on the colour wheel (see opposite page) are called complementaries. For example, blue is the complementary of orange, red of green and yellow of violet. When placed side by side, two complementaries have a powerful effect on each other, the one heightening and intensifying the other. A small patch of red in a large area of green can make both the red and the green look that much brighter. Similarly, blue appears more vibrant with orange nearby. The visual impact of complementary colours is quite considerable and by controlling them carefully in your pictures you can achieve some dramatic results.

The reason this contrast between complementary colours is so effective has to do with the way the human eye works. The cones in the eye which perceive a certain colour have a natural tendency to 'search' for its complementary whenever they are stimulated. You can see this for yourself by carrying out a simple experiment. Stare at a bright red area of colour for 20 seconds, then look away to a sheet of white paper: a green after-image of the object appears. If you reverse the process and start with an area of green, you will see a red after-image. Every colour has its complementary, which can be found in the same way.

Theory into practice

You can make full use of complementary contrast to add zest to your painting. Introduce touches of red or reddish brown into areas of green foliage or grass and you make them look more lively. Complementaries placed side by side form a bright and eye-catching boundary which can be used strategically to draw the eye to the focal point of your composition. To produce luminous shadows, introduce some of the complementary colour of the object into the shadow mixture; for example, an orange will cast a shadow with a bluish tinge, while a red apple will cast a shadow that has a greenish tinge.

Neutral colours

Conversely, if two complementaries are mixed together they neutralize each other and form a whole range of greys which are far more subtle and interesting than the greys mixed from black and white. These neutral greys provide a marvellous foil for brighter, more vibrant colours. They have an inherent harmony and are never strident.

Colours that lie opposite each other on the colour wheel are called complementary colours. When juxtaposed in a painting they intensify each other.

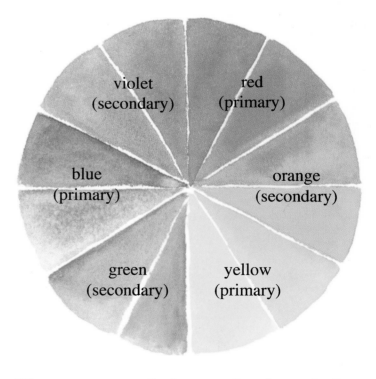

The arrangement of colours on the colour wheel helps the artist understand the relationship between the colours and the effect they have on one another when used together.

Evening Shadow

Our eyes often perceive the shadows in a scene as being the complementary (opposite) colour to that of the illuminated part. Here, the artist has exploited this effect, giving a blue-violet tinge to the shadows on the yellow beach. The violet/ yellow complements are present everywhere in the painting, giving an impression of consistent, harmonious light.

WATERCOLOUR PAINTS IN THE FOLLOWING COLOURS

- *Naples yellow light*
- *Cadmium red*
- *Alizarin crimson*
- *Cadmium yellow*
- *Lemon yellow*
- *Raw sienna*

1 Using thinly diluted lemon yellow, paint the shapes of the deckchairs with the no. 8 brush. Mix a pale flesh tint from thinly diluted lemon yellow and alizarin crimson. Use this to suggest the shapes of the figures and the dog on the sand as simple colour silhouettes, then jot in the figures sitting in the deckchairs. Leave to dry, then add a further wash of flesh tint to model the forms of the figures with light and shade.

2 Paint the evening sky using variegated washes. First, tilt your board at a slight angle and dampen the sky area with water. Using a well-loaded no. 8 brush, apply well-diluted cadmium yellow to the whole area. While this is still damp, float a band of French ultramarine across the top of the paper, and a band of alizarin crimson near the horizon. The colours will gently merge together to create the effect of a hazy sky (see detail). Paint the sea with French ultramarine mixed with just a touch of alizarin crimson, fading the colour with more water in the foreground. When painting variegated washes, it takes a little practice to achieve a smooth transition from one colour to the next. The secret is to load your brush well and work quickly and confidently.

3 Paint the long shadows cast by the deckchairs and figures using French ultramarine, warmed with a touch of alizarin crimson in places. Vary the tones of the shadows, making them lighter the further they are from the objects casting them. Use the no. 4 brush and a darker tone of alizarin and ultramarine to suggest the buckets and spade, and their shadows, on the left of the picture.

Helpful Hint

**WHEN PAINTING FIGURES IN A LAND-
SCAPE, REMEMBER, TOO MUCH DETAIL
RENDERS THEM LIFELESS AND WOODEN.
AIM TO CAPTURE THEIR SHAPES AND
GESTURES SIMPLY AND RAPIDLY.**

4 Now clothe the figures, painting the man's shorts with ultramarine and the woman's swimsuit and sunhat with diluted cadmium red. Let some of the red bleed into the shadow, giving the luminous effect of reflected light. Use the same colours to paint the red and blue stripes on the deckchairs, switching to the no. 8 brush.

5 Switch to the no. 4 brush and paint the colourful parasol with cadmium yellow, cadmium red and ultramarine, using a mixture of all three colours to make a dark mauve for the scalloped edge and the pole. Mix a diluted wash of French ultramarine and paint the shadows of the people sitting in the deckchairs.

6 Now add more detail to the figures sitting on the sand, strengthening the shadows with transparent washes of ultramarine. Mix a dark wash of ultramarine and alizarin crimson and paint the man's hat and the dark tones on the dog.

7 Mix a warm grey from ultramarine and a hint of alizarin crimson and paint the hazy tones of islands in the distance. Now paint the sandy beach with a mixture of raw sienna, cadmium yellow and just a touch of cadmium red, tickling the paint round the shapes of the figures. Strengthen the tone in the foreground with more cadmium red, washing the colour over the cast shadows.

Helpful Hint

WHEN YOU'RE WAITING FOR WASHES TO DRY, USE THE BACK OF YOUR HAND TO TEST FOR DRYNESS. IT IS A MORE SENSITIVE RECEPTOR THAN THE FINGERS AND WON'T LEAVE GREASE MARKS ON THE PAPER.

8 Sketch in a suggestion of the deckchair frames using ultramarine applied with the tip of the no. 4 brush. Add further washes of ultramarine to the cast shadows on the sand, to give an impression of double shadows. Now that the picture has developed, the sky may look a bit 'washed out'; if so, go over it again with the same colours used in step 2 and the no. 8 brush.

9 Use dots and dashes of French ultramarine and alizarin crimson, applied with the no. 4 brush, to suggest groups of people walking along the beach in the distance. Use smaller, sketchier marks for the figures in the water. This dimunition of scale gives the picture a strong sense of receding space. Leave the painting to dry.

10 Check that the painting is completely dry, then add the final touch of sparkling sunlight on the distant sea. To do this, fold a small piece of fine-grade sandpaper and use the folded edge to scrape away some of the dry paint (see detail). Scrape very gently so that paint is removed only from the 'peaks' of the paper grain, leaving a series of broken white highlights. Work in one direction only, so as not to tear the paper.

55

Salting and Scraping

Judy Linnell
WINTER WOODS
By delicately scraping out small patches of colour with fine sandpaper, the artist has not only added texture to the trees but also suggested the sparkle of frost in the air.

Salting

Fascinating effects can be produced by scattering salt crystals into a wet watercolour wash. A little 'star' forms around each crystal as the salt soaks up the paint. Do not sprinkle on too much salt – a few granules is quite sufficient. Leave the painting to dry (this stage requires patience – it can take up to 20 minutes) then gently brush off the salt granules. The pattern of pale, crystalline shapes that remains can be used to suggest anything that your imagination desires. Use salt to add a hint of texture to rocks and stone walls, to suggest wild flowers in a field, to create the effect of falling snow, or simply to enliven a flat wash of colour.

Experiment with salt to discover what you can do with this technique. You will find that bigger, softer shapes are produced by applying salt to a wet wash, whereas smaller, more granular shapes are produced on a damp wash.

Scraping

Once a watercolour wash is dry you can create delicate textures and highlights by scratching or scraping back to the white paper using either a sharp point or a piece of fine-grade sandpaper. Use this technique to suggest, for example, sunlight catching on blades of grass or the frothy foam on incoming waves.

Try also rubbing with a hard eraser to remove just a little colour and create soft highlights – perfect for suggesting shafts of sunlight in the sky.

Teasels and Pollen

Using a number of water-colour techniques, you can render many of the textures of nature, creating some fascinating effects. Here, wet paint is textured with salt grains and dry paint is scraped with fine sandpaper to give a wonderful impression of pollen and seeds borne on the air.

YOU WILL NEED

✔ *Stretched sheet of 140lb (285gsm) Not surface watercolour paper, 17H x 23in (44.4 x 58.4cm)*

✔ *1in (25mm) flat brush*

✔ *No. 12 round brush*

✔ *No. 6 round brush*

✔ *Deep-welled palette or mixing saucers*

✔ *Masking fluid*

✔ *Black fine liner pen*

✔ *Fine sandpaper*

✔ *Drinking straw*

WATERCOLOUR PAINTS IN THE FOLLOWING COLOURS

- *Raw sienna*
- *Cadmium lemon*
- *French ultramarine*
- *Indigo*
- *Light red*
- *Alizarin crimson*

1 To preserve the pale forms of the cow parsley stalks while you paint the dark background, draw in their shapes with a no. 6 round brush and masking fluid (sketch them first in pencil if you feel hesitant). Spatter a few small drops of masking fluid randomly over the paper – these will represent tiny, floating seed heads. Leave to dry for five to 10 minutes. Wash your brush immediately to prevent masking fluid clogging the hairs.

Helpful Hint

SPEED IS OF THE ESSENCE WITH THIS TECHNIQUE, SO IT'S A GOOD IDEA TO PREPARE YOUR WASHES IN ADVANCE SO YOU DON'T HAVE TO STOP AT AN INCONVENIENT MOMENT TO MIX A FRESH BATCH OF COLOUR.

2 Prepare washes for the background tint: a pale yellow (cadmium lemon and raw sienna), a warm grey (French ultramarine and light red) and a cool grey (indigo and alizarin crimson). Wet the whole surface of the paper with clean water, using a 1in (25mm) flat brush. Working quickly, apply the yellow wash with broad, sweeping strokes in a vertical direction, fading the colour out at the top of the paper. Before this dries, randomly drop in washes of warm and cool grey, darkest at the bottom and fading out towards the top with some of the yellow wash showing through. Allow the colours to merge softly on the wet surface. Now sprinkle grains of salt into the wet paint and leave the painting to dry for at least 20 minutes.

3 When dry, shake any excess salt from the paper, revealing a pale, mottled pattern. Paint the feathery, rounded forms of the teasels with a no. 12 round brush and a purplish mix of ultramarine and light red, adding more water for the paler tones. Paint the fine forms of the prickles and drooping tendrils using the tip of a no. 6 round brush. Darken the mixture with more blue for the teasels near the bottom of the painting, which are in shadow. Leave to dry.

4 Here's a novel technique for suggesting twigs and bracken in the background. Apply blots of the dark blue mix here and there along the bottom edge of the paper. Now take a drinking straw, place it near the base of each blot and blow upwards through it, sending spidery tendrils of paint shooting outwards in various directions.

5 When the painting is completely dry, remove all traces of masking fluid from the picture by carefully rubbing it away with a clean fingertip.

Helpful Hint

AFTER STEP 3 THE ARTIST WASN'T HAPPY WITH THE COMPOSITION, SO SHE ADDED ANOTHER TEASEL ON THE RIGHT OF THE PICTURE. REMEMBER TO STEP BACK FROM YOUR PAINTING OCCASIONALLY AND VIEW IT AS A WHOLE, AND BE READY TO CHANGE THINGS IF NECESSARY.

6 Paint in the cow parsley with a light wash of raw sienna applied with a no. 6 round brush, leaving slivers of white paper for the highlights. The warmth of the sienna provides a pleasing contrast with the cool blue hues in the rest of the painting. Leave to dry.

7 Use a black fine liner pen to enhance the edges of the cow parsley stalks and give them further definition. This also ensures that the cow parsley comes forward in the picture plane, giving the picture a sense of perspective. Pick out the star-shaped bracts at the ends of the stalks with the fine liner pen.

8 Continue working with the pen to pick out the prickles and the tendrils on the teasels. With a small piece of fine sandpaper, gently remove the surface layer of paint on the tops of the teasels and in parts of the background to introduce light and create texture. Ensure that the paper is dry before you do this or it will tear.

Helpful Hint

KEEP A SMALL PIECE OF WATER-COLOUR PAPER HANDY TO TEST THE MIXTURE AND STRENGTHS OF COLOURS BEFORE COMMITTING THEM TO YOUR PAINTING. BEAR IN MIND THAT WATERCOLOUR BECOMES LIGHTER WHEN DRY THAN WHEN IT APPEARS WET.

9 Mix a dull green from a mixture of French ultramarine and raw sienna to shade the stems of the cow parsley and give them three-dimensional form. Now stand back to assess the painting and check that it is working well as a whole. If necessary, add more detail with the pen – but don't overdo it. The appeal of this image lies in its delicate, 'lost and found' quality.

Painting Sunsets

Trevor Chamberlain
DUSTY SHEEP-TRACK, EVENING
A beautiful portrayal of evening light, captured with soft, wet–in–wet washes of translucent colour on a fairly absorbent paper.

Sunsets and evening skies, with their rich, glowing colours, have long been a popular subject for artists. Anyone in search of inspiration need look no further than the work of the English artist JMW Turner, whose glorious studies of sunsets seem to glow with an inner light.

Painting outdoors

If you are painting outdoors and trying to capture the glowing effects of the evening sky, you need to work quickly as the light changes and fades rapidly at this time of day. To save time, get to your chosen spot before sunset and have all your equipment set out ready.

In this situation, the key is to simplify both colours and forms so that you can quickly convey the mood and atmosphere as it appears before you. Work on a small scale and use large brushes to apply broad strokes of transparent colour – small brushes can result in a tight, overworked image. Choose a limited range of colours to work with – you won't have time to dither over which colours to mix once the sun starts to go down.

Another approach is to make on-the-spot sketches in pastel or gouache and use these as reference for a painting to be completed at home. Work with just a few principal colours on a mid-toned paper, which leaves you free to concentrate on the lights and darks.

The sky at sunset takes on a radiant glow which even the brightest pigment colours cannot hope to match. The artist, therefore, must use cunning and skill in order to create the illusion of radiant light in his or her painting. One way to do this is by introducing cool colours as well as warm into the sky, because warm colours appear brighter and more intense when placed next to cool colours. When you interweave the warm pinks and golds of the setting sun with the cool blues and violets of the clouds, these warm and cool colours 'vibrate'

against each other and create a radiant glow. In addition, the cool, shadowy tones in the darkening landscape will enhance the warmth in the sky.

When faced with a glorious sunset the temptation can sometimes be to mix too many strong pinks, oranges and reds so that when completed the sky seems to jump forward and hang in front of the landscape below. The secret of success is to use 'hot' colours sparingly. Exercise restraint with your brushwork and be selective with your colours. When painting the sun itself, for example, an orb of pale, soft colour will look subtler and more evocative than one painted in garishly bright colours.

Robert Tilling
EVENING LIGHT
Here the magical effect of a luminous evening sky reflected on still water is powerfully conveyed by paring the image down to its essential elements.

Sunset over the Lagoon

The changing hues of a sky at sunset are a richly evocative subject for the watercolour artist. This view of Venice captures that magical time of day, just before the sun sinks, when the sky takes on a luminous glow and the tones of the buildings are reduced to dark, shadowy forms.

WATERCOLOUR PAINTS IN THE FOLLOWING COLOURS

- *French ultramarine*
- *Prussian blue*
- *Cadmium yellow*
- *Cadmium red*
- *Lemon yellow*
- *Ivory black*
- *Alizarin crimson*
- *Burnt sienna*
- *Payne's gray*
- *Permanent white gouache paint*

1 Sketch in the main outlines of the composition using an HB pencil. Paint the sky with thinly diluted washes of colour applied wet-into-wet with a no. 10 brush and broad, uneven brushstrokes. Start at the top with French ultramarine, then use various combinations of ultramarine, Prussian blue and just a touch of cadmium yellow to make pale grey-blues. Add touches of thinly diluted permanent white here and there to suggest soft white clouds. Mix permanent white with a little cadmium red for the pink sky above the horizon.

Helpful Hint

THE BUFF-COLOURED INGRES PAPER USED HERE PROVIDES A USEFUL MID TONE ON WHICH TO WORK. IF YOU PREFER TO USE NORMAL WATERCOLOUR PAPER TINT IT WITH A WEAK WASH OF BURNT SIENNA.

2 Switch to a no. 4 brush and loosely block in the distant line of buildings. The colours used here are cadmium red, lemon yellow, burnt sienna, ultramarine and ivory black, with touches of permanent white. Mix these in different combinations and allow the colours to run into each other to achieve a wide range of tones, from purple-grey through to a warm brown.

3 Let the underwashes dry, then mix a dark grey from ultramarine and black and suggest windows and doorways on the buildings. These are quite a long way distant, so don't overdo the detailing. Here you can see how loosely the paint is applied – yet there is enough detail to describe the character of the old Venetian buildings.

4 Now start to paint the water, starting with a thin wash of white, lemon yellow and a hint of ultramarine for the stretch of pale green water in the distance. Mix white, alizarin crimson and a touch of lemon yellow for the pink areas to show the reflection of the setting sun, and white and ultramarine for the blue areas. Apply the colours with a no. 10 brush using short, curving brushstrokes to suggest the choppy surface of the water.

5 Check that the sky washes are dry, then mix ultramarine and alizarin and put in the dark storm clouds. Use a no. 4 brush and apply the paint wash-over-wash with lively, energetic strokes to give form and movement to the clouds. Now paint the light sky behind the buildings with narrow bands of white tinged with alizarin. Mix cadmium red and lemon yellow for the orange glow.

6 Build up the density of tone in the storm clouds with a darker wash of ultramarine and alizarin. Use loose, curving strokes to give the impression of movement and to give energy to the painting. Add a thin wash of white to the sky just above the buildings to lighten it. Switch to a no. 10 brush and paint the sky above the storm clouds with a loose wash of white gouache and ultramarine.

7 Now you can put in the fiery sunset colours. Mix lemon yellow, cadmium red and a little white to make a rich golden orange and, with the tip of a no. 4 brush, add touches of this colour around the lower edges of the clouds. For the yellow-tinted clouds, use flecks of lemon yellow and white, warmed with a hint of cadmium red in places. The detail (right) reveals the variety of brushwork and colour the artist has used in the sky. The airy, vaporous quality of the thin clouds at the top is described using dry paint, dragged on with a dry brush to create ragged strokes. These strokes cut into the edges of the storm clouds, giving them a more natural, broken edge.

8 Deepen the tones on the distant buildings with a mixture of Payne's gray and white. Mix lemon yellow, ultramarine and white and suggest the architectural detailing on the nearer buildings on the right. Suggest the distant rooftops with thinly diluted burnt sienna.

9 Switch to a no. 1 brush and paint the sun's reflection on the water with dark, medium and light tones mixed from cadmium red, lemon yellow and white. Use the tip of the brush to make rhythmic strokes that suggest the way the reflection is broken up by the moving surface. To enhance the effect of space and perspective, make these strokes smaller and more closely spaced in the distance.

Suggest the steps leading down into the water with light and dark tones of burnt sienna and black. When dry, dilute the colours with more water and paint the wooden mooring poles emerging from the water.

10 Finally, paint the reflections of the mooring poles with broken, swirling strokes, using a dark tone of ultramarine and Payne's gray. Lighten the wash with more water and use it to paint the dark ripples on the water's surface. To further enhance the illusion of receding space, jot in the groups of wooden mooring poles just visible in the distant water.

Painting Flowers

It is easy to see why flowers are such a popular painting subject. Not only are they a delight to the eye, with their graceful forms and gorgeous colours, but you can select and arrange them to your liking and paint them at your leisure – at least until the blooms die!

Setting up

Try to keep the arrangement of your flowers simple and informal – a fussy arrangement tends to look stiff and unnatural. Arrange the blooms so that they fan out naturally and gracefully, allowing some to overlap others. Place them at different heights, with some of the heads viewed from the back or in profile, just as they would appear if they were growing in a garden. Also be mindful of colour. Simple colour harmonies are usually more effective than garish multicolour arrangements.

Techniques

Try not to get bogged down in describing each leaf and flower in exact botanical detail; think of your vase of flowers as a single form in itself and establish the broad areas of colour and tone first. Starting from this base you can then build up gradually to the smaller details.

The pure translucency of watercolours makes them ideal for capturing the delicate quality of leaves and petals. Plan your approach carefully, first deciding which highlights need to be 'reserved' as white paper and then building up methodically from the palest to the darkest tones. Delicate overlapping washes can produce the effects of light shining on and through petals, and so can working wet-in-wet, allowing one colour to spread into another so that there are no hard edges. Avoid heavy applications of colour – thin, transparent washes allow light to reflect off the white paper and up through the colours.

Lost and found edges

When you paint a vase of flowers, try to convey an impression of some of the blooms being further back than others. Do this by bringing the nearer flowers into sharp focus while playing down those towards the back of the group. Pick out one or two flowers near the front and emphasize these with crisp 'found' edges. Make the flowers further back less well defined by using soft, 'lost' edges and more muted colours. Let some of the flowers touch and overlap to create the illusion of three dimensions.

Shirley Trevena
BOB'S RED TULIPS
Left: *Because a vase or jug is a tall, narrow shape you will often need some additional objects to provide balance.*

Sally Keir
IRIS 'WARM GOLD'
Below: *Gouache paints have a vibrant light-reflecting quality that is ideally suited to painting flowers.*

Lilies and Ivy

A huge bouquet of lilies makes a spectacular subject to paint in watercolour. The artist has taken great care with the arrangement, ensuring that the flowers, leaves and stems set up linear rhythms that lead the eye around the picture. The ivy falling in elegant curves around the vase helps to balance the weight of the flowers.

YOU WILL NEED

✔ Stretched sheet of Not surface watercolour paper, 16½ x 23in (41.9 x 58.4cm)

✔ No. 3 round brush

✔ No. 6 round brush

✔ HB pencil

✔ Kneaded eraser

✔ Soft tissues

WATERCOLOUR PAINTS IN THE FOLLOWING COLOURS

● *French ultramarine*
● *Mauve*
● *Purple madder alizarin*
● *Carmine*
● *Alizarin crimson*
● *Bright red*
● *Chrome yellow*
● *Sap green*

1 Make a careful outline drawing of the flower arrangement using an HB pencil. Start by working on the glass vase, using the no. 3 brush. Suggest the shadowy tones in the water with varying mixes of French ultramarine and mauve. Put on colour, water it down and spread it, then take some colour off again with a wet brush to create a range of subtle tones. For the leaves and stems use sap green and chrome yellow, cooled with hints of ultramarine and mauve. Leave to dry completely.

2 Lightly wash over the topmost lily flowers with a pale wash of carmine, leaving the centres unpainted. Then add a little mauve to give form, letting the colours merge softly on the damp paper. Apply chrome yellow to the centres of the flowers, then add a little sap green to the mix and paint the stamens. Start to paint the surrounding leaves using the same mix, adding a little French ultramarine for the darker tones. When the lily petals are dry, use the tip of the brush to add dots of purple madder alizarin for the spots on the petals.

Helpful Hint
THESE INITIAL COLOURS TOP AND BOTTOM WILL GIVE YOU SOME IDEA OF THE INTENSITY OF TONES TO BE USED WITHIN THE OVERALL PICTURE.

3 Work on the two unopened flowers at the top right, using the same greens mixed in step 1 for the stalks and leaves. Paint the closed flower buds with delicate washes of carmine, adding a hint of palest green from your palette. Add touches of bright red for the deeper tones. The colours will merge softly on the damp paper.

4 Continue painting in the flowers and foliage as before, working all around the picture so that the overall balance of colour and tone can be judged as you work. Mix and blend the colours on the paper, wet-into-wet, to describe the delicate forms of the petals (see detail). Strengthen your washes with more colour or dilute them with water to vary the tones and suggest the play of light on the flowers. Add some shadowy tones between the flowers and among the stems above the water in the vase with ultramarine and purple madder alizarin.

This detail of a flower (left) reveals the delicate translucency of the washes. The artist applies deeper pink hues of carmine and alizarin crimson in the centres of the flowers, washing the colour out more as she moves down the length of the petals and leaving flecks of white paper for the highlights.

5 Paint the unopened flower buds to the top left of the picture with delicate washes of chrome yellow, adding a faint blush of carmine wet-into-wet. Continue filling in the flowers and foliage around the edges of the arrangement using the same colour mixes as before. Mix a cool, bluish green with ultramarine and a little sap green and carmine for the leaves that are in shadow.

6 Develop the woody flower stems in the vase with crisp washes and glazes of sap green and carmine, adding touches of purple madder alizarin for the darker stems. Leave to dry, then work up the shadows in the water with transparent overlaid washes of ultramarine, sap green and purple madder alizarin. Lift off colour with a wet brush to lighten some of the tones. Using a tissue, blot the wash here and there around the points where the flower stems break through the surface of the water. Mix sap green and carmine for the brownish stems of the trailing ivy.

7 Paint the ivy leaves using sap green, adding a little bright red for the darker leaves. Use the no. 6 brush to paint the background around the vase with variegated washes of ultramarine and purple madder alizarin. Apply the paint loosely, leaving chinks of white paper showing through to give sparkle and suggest dappled light and shade. Dip your brush in water and lift out some of the colour so that the wash fades out almost to nothing at the extreme edges of the picture.

8 Now mix a watery solution of ultramarine and fill in the rest of the background, blotting off any excess colour with a tissue. Use the no. 3 brush for the intricate shapes between the flowers and stems. Add a little purple madder alizarin here and there to create subtle nuances of shade.

9 Suggest the shadows cast by the flowers onto the table with deeper washes of ultramarine and purple madder alizarin. Apply the paint with loose, rapid brushstrokes, leaving chinks of the pale underwash showing through. Soften some of the shadows further back with water.

Helpful Hint

DON'T WORRY IF YOU APPEAR TO HAVE USED TOO MUCH COLOUR, SIMPLY APPLY MORE WATER, WASH THE COLOUR OUT AND THEN DAB OFF THE EXCESS WITH A PIECE OF CRUMPLED TISSUE.

10 Use the no. 3 brush and the appropriate colours to strengthen and define any details that may have become overshadowed by the background. Darken the background behind the flowers to 'throw' them forward and give them more definition. Leave the painting to dry completely, then gently rub over the surface with a kneaded eraser to remove any of the remaining pencil lines and to soften and lighten the overall effect of the petals.

Decorative Patterns

Penny Quested
THE SITTING ROOM
This delightful water-colour is reminiscent of the paintings of Henri Matisse. The artist has deliberately stylized the subject to stress the patterned quality of the objects in the room, eliminating most of the modelling in favour of all-over decorative impact.

Most still-life compositions are rendered realistically, using light, shade and perspective to produce a three-dimensional effect. Sometimes, however, it can be more entertaining to deliberately exaggerate or simplify your subject in order to create an exciting and original image – for example, treating it simply as a flat, two-dimensional pattern of shapes and colours.

Many of the domestic items artists assemble for still-life painting – containers, ornaments and fabrics – contain a wealth of colour and pattern elements which can be explored for their own sake. When setting up a decorative still life, it is important to ensure that shapes,

colours and patterns combine to create a unified, harmonious effect. Think about the relationship of one object to another, and try to introduce interesting lines and rhythms that lead the eye around the painting.

Using gouache paints

The project painting which follows was painted with gouache paints, which are an opaque form of watercolour. The opacity of gouache gives strong, bright hues, and because the paint dries with a matt, smooth, opaque surface, it is ideal for this decorative style of painting in which bold, vibrant colours are placed side by side with minimal modelling.

YOU WILL NEED

- ✔ Sheet of 140lb (285gsm) Not surface watercolour paper 20 x 15in (50.8 x 38.1cm)
- ✔ No. 7 round brush
- ✔ No. 3 round brush
- ✔ HB pencil

Souvenir of India

By emphasizing bright colours and simplifying shapes, the artist has drawn attention to the decorative quality of this subject. The colours of the various objects have been carefully chosen to harmonize with and complement one another.

GOUACHE PAINTS IN THE FOLLOWING COLOURS

- Indigo
- Brilliant violet
- Permanent white
- Prussian blue
- Rose malmaison
- Ivory black
- Alizarin crimson
- Yellow ochre
- Brilliant yellow
- Bistre
- Lemon yellow
- Winsor green

1 Make a careful outline drawing of the still life using an HB pencil. Make sure that your drawing adequately fills your sheet of paper, otherwise it will look as though it is 'floating'.

2 Begin by painting the anemones with the no. 7 brush, using a mixture of brilliant violet, permanent white and a touch of indigo, diluted with water. Use the same colour to put in the wavy pattern on the decorative tile. Add shade and tone to the petals with a mix of indigo and brilliant violet.

3 Mix Prussian blue, rose malmaison and a little ivory black to create a deep purple for the centres of the anemones. Continue working with this mixture, putting in the dark areas of the patterned scarf. You build up this picture by blocking in each individual area with paint, as if it were a two-dimensional pattern.

4 Mix a pale blue wash with cobalt blue, permanent white and a hint of yellow ochre for the blue bands on the tall flower vase. Add more cobalt blue to the mixture and paint the dots on the bands. Now use this mixture to paint the mid-blue areas on the scarf.

5 Use a mix of rose malmaison and white to paint the lilies, varying the amounts of white to develop the tones. Use brilliant yellow for the centres. Paint the pink patterns on the scarf and on the elephant carving with the same mixtures. Add a little brilliant yellow to the mix to make a pale orange and paint the flowers on the small vase and the orange bands on the taller vase. Deepen the mix with more rose malmaison and brilliant yellow to make a deeper orange for the floral pattern on the scarf.

6 Make a very pale, neutral-coloured wash from yellow ochre, cobalt blue and white, thinly diluted. Apply this to the small vase and the decorative tile, working around the shape of the elephant. Add a little indigo to the wash and paint the shadow inside the rim of the vase and on the edge of the tile.

Helpful Hint
SOME GOUACHE COLOURS TEND TO SEPARATE AFTER THE MIX HAS BEEN STANDING A WHILE IN THE PALETTE. SO BEFORE YOU USE A MIX, GIVE IT A STIR WITH YOUR BRUSH.

7 Switch to the no. 3 brush and use a lighter version of the same wash to paint the crackled effect on the surface of the tile with a series of criss-crossed lines.

8 Mix a pale yellow with rose malmaison, brilliant yellow and white and apply this to the large vase with the no. 7 brush, leaving the birds and flowers white. Now mix lemon yellow, Winsor green, white and a touch of cobalt blue to make a pale green, and paint the stems and leaves of the flowers with the no. 3 brush. Mix in a little rose malmaison for the stems, varying their hues from green to pinkish green. Darken the wash with indigo for the shadows and the veins on the leaves.

9 Touch in the bright colours on the elephant carving with brilliant yellow and a bright green mix of Winsor green and lemon yellow. On the tall vase, use brilliant yellow on the birds and flower and mix Winsor green and yellow ochre for the leaf motif. Mix rose malmaison and yellow ochre for the elephant motif on the tile. Then mix a dark green from Winsor green and Prussian blue and paint the leaf pattern on the small vase and the green patterns on the tile and the scarf.

10 Paint the red details on the elephant carving with rose malmaison. Then add Prussian blue to the mix to make a deeper red for the flowers on the small jug and the detailing on the elephant on the tile. Use the same colour to emphasize and outline the floral pattern on the scarf with sketchy lines.

Helpful Hint
DON'T BE PUT OFF BY THE SEEMINGLY COMPLEX PATTERNS IN THIS STILL LIFE: SIMPLIFY THEM AS YOU PAINT.

11 Fill in the body on the elephant carving with a diluted grey wash of cobalt blue, brilliant yellow and white. Mix bistre with brilliant violet to make a rich brown and complete the decorative pattern on the tall vase. Use the same mix on the handle of the small vase.

12 To finish, mix Prussian blue with ivory black and paint the linear details on the tile. Outline the elephant carving with the same mixture and paint in its features and details. Stand back and assess the painting. The vibrant colours should enhance the richly patterned subject, with no one area of the painting being more important than the rest.

Texturing

Jane Strother
ITALIAN HOUSE
There are lots of ways in which watercolour paint can be used to create textures and effects. Here, the artist has used the spattering technique to suggest the crumbling, pitted stonework of the old building. To spatter, load an old toothbrush with paint, hold it above the paper, then draw your thumbnail through the bristles to release a shower of fine droplets.

One of the more unusual techniques you can try with watercolour is texturing with plastic wrap – the thin sort used for wrapping food. This process is very simple and produces extraordinary and unpredictable effects. In our project painting the artist has used plastic wrap to create an impression of the ripples and eddies on the surface of a pond, but it could equally be used to add interest to a sky or to suggest the dappled shadows beneath a tree – the possibilities are limited only by the extent of your imagination.

The paint has to be wet for this technique to work, so have everything you need to hand so that you can work quickly. Decide on the area you want to texture and stretch a sheet of thin plastic food wrap over it. Wrap the plastic round the back of the board if necessary, to keep it taut. Using the tips of your fingers, press and squeeze the plastic so that it wrinkles up and forms ridges. With the plastic still in place, lay the board flat and leave the painting to dry. This can take anything from 30 minutes to several hours, depending on how big an area you are painting and how much wet paint you have applied.

When you think the paint looks dry, peel away the plastic. Where the paint has become trapped in the folds of the plastic, it dries with an attractive striated pattern with subtle variations in tone.

Three Fishes

The use of unortho-
dox methods is fun
and demonstrates
the creative potential
of the watercolour
medium. In this
delightful painting
the artist exploits
the fluid, unpre-
dictable nature of
watercolour, working
into the wet paint
with crumpled plas-
tic wrap to create
the patterns in the
water.

YOU WILL NEED

✓ *Sheet of 140lb (285gsm) Not surface watercolour paper, 16½ x 22in (41.9 x 55.8cm)*

✓ *No. 16 round brush*

✓ *No. 4 round brush*

✓ *Sheet of thin plastic wrap*

✓ *Table salt*

✓ *Gum arabic*

WATERCOLOUR PAINTS IN THE FOLLOWING COLOURS

- *Winsor blue*
- *Winsor green*
- *Cadmium yellow*
- *Cadmium red*
- *Alizarin crimson*
- *French ultramarine*
- *Permanent white gouache paint*

1 Mix a watery solution of cadmium yellow. Working directly onto the paper, paint the shapes of the three fishes with a well-loaded no. 16 round brush. Work quickly and confidently with just a few brushstrokes, using the belly of the brush for the wide bodies and tapering down to the tails with the tip of the brush.

Helpful Hint
IF YOU ARE UNSURE ABOUT 'DRAWING' WITH THE BRUSH, LIGHTLY DRAW THE FISHES IN PENCIL FIRST.

2 Strengthen the tones on the fishes with further washes of cadmium yellow. While the paint is still damp, mix cadmium yellow and cadmium red to make a rich orange and quickly brush this over the fishes' bodies to give them form and shading. Let the orange washes merge into the underwash, suggesting the softly rounded bodies of the fish. Use the tip of the brush and long, sweeping strokes to paint the fins and tails, lifting the brush as you near the end of each stroke to create ragged marks that suggest movement.

3 Develop the form of the fish on the right using alizarin crimson, darkened with French ultramarine for the deepest tones on the fins, tail and body. Define the eye and the shape of the head with the tip of the brush. While the paint is still wet, sprinkle a few grains of salt along the fish's body and leave to dry for at least 10 minutes (see inset). When dry, brush off the salt to reveal a pattern resembling fish scales. Dip the brush in clean water and work around the outline of the fish to soften the colour – this creates an impression of the fish moving through the water.

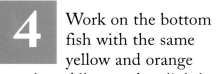

4 Work on the bottom fish with the same yellow and orange washes. Allow to dry slightly, then paint the eyes and the dark markings on the back with a mix of cadmium red and French ultramarine. Build up the mottled pattern with further washes, applied wet on dry. Then sprinkle a little salt into the wet paint and leave to dry as before.

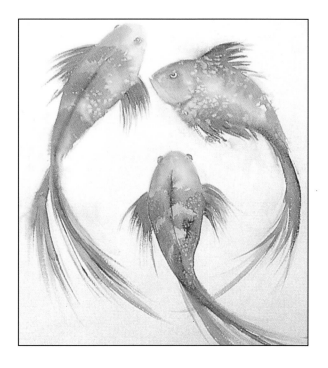

5 Now paint the lefthand fish in exactly the same way, this time mixing alizarin crimson with just a little ultramarine for the mottled markings. Again, soften the outlines in places to create a suitably 'watery' feel.

6 Now for the fun part. Apply clean water to the background around the fishes and apply broad strokes of Winsor green and Winsor blue to the wet paper to represent the water. Sweep the brush over the fishes' bodies in places, so they appear to be in the water. Sprinkle a few grains of salt near the top of the picture, and around the fishes' tails and fins. Before the paint has chance to dry, stretch thin plastic wrap horizontally over the entire picture. Pull and push the plastic with your fingers, as shown. Leave to dry for at least 30 minutes.

7 Peel away a corner of the plastic wrap and check that the paint is completely dry. If it is, remove the plastic wrap from the whole picture. Brush away the salt granules. Here you can see the result: where the paint gets trapped in the folds of the plastic, it dries with crisp, hard outlines that look like ripples and eddies on the surface of the water. The mottled patterns formed by the salt represent tiny bubbles in the water created by the fishes' movement.

Helpful Hint

YOU HAVE TO WORK QUICKLY WITH THIS TECHNIQUE – THE PAINT MUST BE WET WHEN YOU APPLY THE SALT AND THE PLASTIC WRAP. IF YOU'RE WORKING ON A LARGE SCALE, COMPLETE THE TOP HALF OF THE PITCURE FIRST AND THEN REPEAT THE EXERCISE FOR THE BOTTOM HALF.

8 Strengthen the tones on the fishes' tails and fins with a mixture of ultramarine and alizarin crimson. Switch to a no. 4 round brush and use the same colour to strengthen details such as the eyes, and the mouth of the righthand fish.

9 Build up more textural detail on the righthand fish, suggesting the scales on its belly with overlaid strokes of alizarin crimson darkened with a hint of ultramarine. Mix a warm gold using cadmium yellow and a hint of cadmium red, adding a little permanent white gouache to give it body. Add strokes of this colour along the fish's back. Allow these washes to dry, then add dots of white gouache for the highlights.

10 Leave the painting to dry completely, then brush a thin layer of gum arabic over the surface of the painting using the no. 10 brush. The gum arabic acts as a kind of varnish and gives an added brightness to the colours, appropriate to the subject.

Painting Stormy Weather

David Curtis
**RAINY MORNING ON THE
RIALTO, VENICE**
**Here the artist has made use of glistening high-
lights reflected on the wet ground, the rooftops
and the awnings to recreate the atmosphere of a
sudden rain shower.**

The sheer power and drama of a storm make it
one of the most challenging weather conditions
for an artist to tackle. Though it is possible to
recreate a stormy scene from photographs (this
was the case with our project painting), there is
no substitute for actually getting out there

among the elements. Other senses apart from
sight have a part to play in painting; if you can
hear the pounding of surf against rocks, or feel
the tension in the air just before a storm breaks,
these qualities will come through in your painting almost without your being aware of it.

Turner was a great believer in braving the elements to paint stormy scenes on the spot. Even
in a blizzard or a downpour, it is possible for less
hardy souls to work directly from nature by
viewing the scene from a car window, or finding
some other shelter. Alternatively you could make
quick, on-the-spot sketches in pencil or watercolour and use these later as reference for a
painting done in the comfort of your home.

Painting methods

Storms can come and go in a matter of minutes, so you have to learn to work rapidly and
intuitively, allowing the paint itself to suggest
the power and drama of nature. Depict rain and
swirling clouds by applying heavy washes and
letting them merge wet-in-wet on damp paper.
Try tilting the board at an angle so that the
colour drifts down towards the horizon, giving
an effect of veils of rain in the distance. When
painting rapidly, wet-into-wet, your washes may
settle unevenly in places; resist the temptation
to eliminate every imperfection, however –
blotches and blooms can be wonderfully sugges-
tive of storm clouds and crashing waves.

By using a dry brush and dragging the
colour lightly over a rough-surfaced paper you
can create lively, broken strokes that convey the
impression of sea foam or wisps of cloud scud-
ding across the sky. Use sweeping, irregular
strokes that reflect the violent, erratic movement of clouds and waves and encourage the
eye to move freely around the picture.

Sea and Sky

In this unusual composition the brooding sky and crashing surf have been deliberately exaggerated in order to capture the powerful drama of a storm at sea. Wet-in-wet washes suggest the constant shifting of clouds, light and water.

YOU WILL NEED

- ✔ Sheet of stretched Not surface watercolour paper, 15 x 22in (38.1 x 55.8cm)
- ✔ Large wash brush
- ✔ ½in (13mm) flat brush
- ✔ No. 2 round brush
- ✔ No. 0 round brush
- ✔ Small, old brush to apply masking fluid
- ✔ Masking fluid
- ✔ HB pencil
- ✔ Mixing saucers
- ✔ Soft tissues

WATERCOLOUR PAINTS IN THE FOLLOWING COLOURS

- ● French ultramarine
- ● Cyanine blue
- ● Cadmium red
- ● Burnt sienna

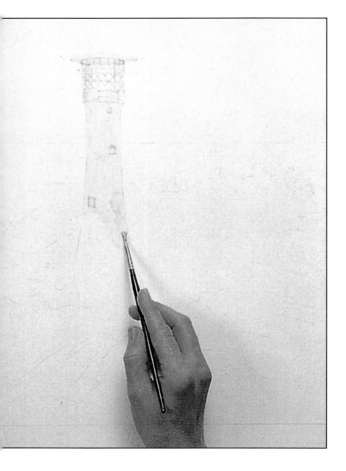

1 Use an HB pencil to sketch in the horizon line, the lighthouse and the outline shape of the foreground breaker. Use masking fluid and an old brush (use a small round one) to block out the shape of the lighthouse and the white breakers in the distance; this allows you to paint the sea and the sky with bold, sweeping strokes, without worrying about the paint running over the edges of your drawing.

2 Mix a wash of cyanine blue and a little ultramarine, heavily diluted with water. With your board tilted at a slight angle, paint the top part of the sky using a large wash brush, working around the top edge of the clouds. If a rill of paint forms at the base of the wash, simply dry off your brush and use it to blot up the excess.

3 Work down the paper with the blue wash, painting the lower half of the sky and then the blue parts of the water. Leave the large foreground breaker white for now. Mix a watery but strong solution of French ultramarine and cadmium red and paint the heavy, purple rain clouds, spreading the paint across the paper with broad brushstrokes. Rinse your brush and blot the edges of the clouds to create soft gradations of colour that suggest mist and rain.

4 While the purple washes are still damp, add further washes in places to deepen the colour. Don't be tempted to smooth out the brushstrokes, but allow the paint to settle unevenly, creating the effect of brooding storm clouds.

5 Mix a watery but strong solution of cyanine blue, ultramarine and touches of cadmium red and apply washes of varying tone over the distant sea with a 1/2in (13mm) flat brush. Now paint the trough of the foreground breaker, spreading the colour upwards from the bottom of the picture with rhythmic strokes to capture the upward force of the water. As with the sky, allow the paint to form into pools and curdled patterns - they add to the dynamic power and force of the wave.

6 Add more pigment to the wash to strengthen it and continue developing the dark shadows in the trough of the breaker. To show the gradation of the sea water as it turns to foam, add water to the edges of the brushstrokes to fade out the colour. The frothy foam on the crest of the breaker is produced with flecked strokes, made by using a small amount of paint on a dry brush and dragging it lightly across the paper with an upward movement. To suggest the dramatic spray as the breaker crashes against the rocks, soften the edge of the blue wash with a wet brush and gently blot with a small piece of crumpled tissue, as shown.

7 With the corner of an eraser, remove the masking fluid from the lighthouse and distant waves. Quickly run over the outline of the lighthouse with a clean, damp no. 2 round brush, to soften the hard edges created by the masking fluid. Now mix a dilute wash of burnt sienna and ultramarine and paint the wall of the lighthouse, starting very pale at the top and becoming darker towards the bottom. Using a no. 0 round brush, paint the detailing at the top of the lighthouse with various greys. Then paint the dark windows with a deep tone of burnt sienna and ultramarine.

8 Stand back and assess your painting so far. Here, the artist decided to accentuate the reflection of the thunderous sky in the choppy sea by adding a wash of ultramarine and cadmium red to the white waves near the horizon. This also increases the illusion of distance, with the waves becoming greyer as they recede towards the horizon.

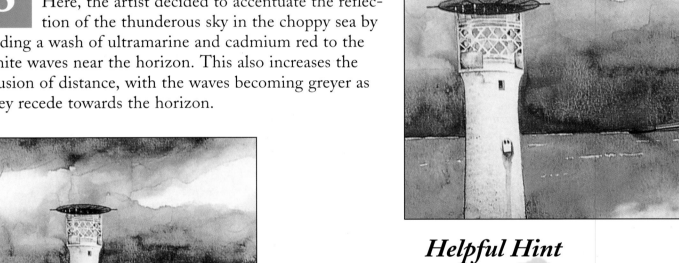

Helpful Hint

THE MARKS SEEN IN THE SKY IN STEP 4 ARE KNOW AS 'BLOOMS' OR 'BACKRUNS'. THEY ARE USUALLY ACCIDENTAL, OCCURRING WHEN YOU WORK INTO A WASH BEFORE IT IS COMPLETELY, DRY; HOWEVER, THEY CAN BE USED DELIBERATELY TO PRODUCE TEXTURES AND EFFECTS THAT WOULD BE DIFFICULT TO CREATE WITH CONVENTIONAL BRUSHWORK.

9 Finally, paint in the rock to the left of the lighthouse with a dark mix of burnt sienna and ultramarine. In the finished painting you will notice that the crashing surf in the foreground consists largely of white paper, its luminosity enhanced by the dark tones of the surrounding sea and sky.

Index

INDEX